A Boy, a Budget, and a Dream

by JASMINE PAUL

illustrated by JOSE NIETO

Copyright © 2020 by Jasmine A. Paul

All rights reserved. No part of this book may be reproduced or transmitted in any form or by any means, electronic or mechanical, including photocopying, recording, or by any information storage and retrieval system, without permission in writing from the copyright owner.

www.createfinstew.com

The information contained in this book is provided as is without warranty of any kind, neither implied nor express, including but not limited to the implied warranties of suitability for a particular purpose. You should consult with a professional where appropriate. The author, editor, illustrator, and designer of this work shall in no event be liable for any damages or losses including, without limitation, direct, indirect, special, punitive, incidental or consequential damages resulting from or caused by this book or its content, including, without limitation, any error, omission, or defect.

Library of Congress Control Number: 2020911092

Illustrations by Jose Nieto
Cover & Layout by Praise Saflor

Publisher's Cataloging-in-Publication Data

Names: Paul, Jasmine A., author. | Nieto, Jose, illustrator.
Title: A Boy , a budget , and a dream / written by Jasmine A. Paul ; illustrated by Jose' Nieto.
Description: Tampa, FL: CreateFinStew LLC, 2021. | Summary: Joey hasn't saved enough money to pay for something he's been dreaming about. Now his only option is to ask his sister for help.
Identifiers: LCCN: 2020911092 | ISBN: 978-1-7334538-2-0 (Hardcover) | 978-1-7334538-3-7 (pbk.)
Subjects: LCSH Siblings--Juvenile fiction. | Brothers and sisters--Juvenile fiction. | Children--Finance, Personal--Juvenile fiction. | Money--Juvenile fiction. | Saving and investment--Juvenile fiction. | African Americans--Juvenile fiction. | CYAC Siblings--Fiction. | Brothers and sisters--Fiction. | Children--Finance, Personal--Fiction. | Money--Fiction. | Saving and investment--Fiction. | African Americans--Fiction. | BISAC JUVENILE FICTION / Concepts / Money | JUVENILE FICTION / Family / Siblings | JUVENILE FICTION / Social Themes / Values & Virtues
Classification: LCC PZ7.1.P3772 Boy 2021 | DDC [E]--dc23

To my siblings, my parents, family, friends and readers. Here's to all of us making the world a more financially healthy place!

- JP

"Who, me?" asks Joey, turning to stare at his sister.

"You're such a dreamer," says Kass. She looks at her computer screen and giggles. Her savings account is growing, and that makes Kass very happy.

"Another 5 dollars! Cha-ching!"

Kass saves her allowance each week. Joey spends most of his! Dad can see that Kass's total is increasing, but Joey isn't doing as well.

Joey is busy daydreaming about a new video game that he's planning to buy. "Let's see," he says. "Mom and dad give us each 5 dollars a week. Then they add a 10 dollar bonus every 4 weeks if we do our chores. So, if I don't spend it all, that means I'll have 30 dollars in my account. Man! I can buy the next Dino Rumble game, a new poster, that cool T-Shirt I saw online, and STEM camp!"

Kass strolls by with her pristine, mint-condition JazzCam Instant Camera and snaps another picture of Joey. It instantly comes out of the camera. SNAP!

"Kass, how did you get that camera, anyway?" Joey asks. "I saved my allowance, created a plan and earned enough money. Then Mom took me to the store to buy it!"

"I need that camera," he wails.

"With what money?" asks Kass. "Did you even check your account today? With your spending habit, you'll have to save your allowance for years and sell everything in your room before you'll be able to buy this camera."

Joey forgot to check his balance this week, so he rushes to the computer and logs in to his account. "I'll show Kass!" he thinks, "I have lots of money."

Then...

Joey looks at his account and sadly realizes that he has a balance of...
only 12 dollars. *Gulp!*

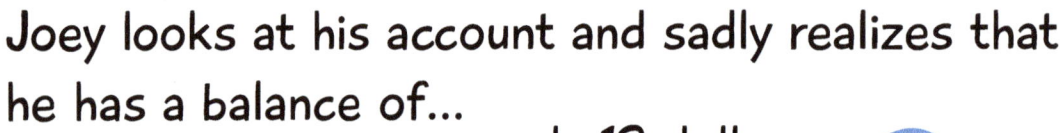

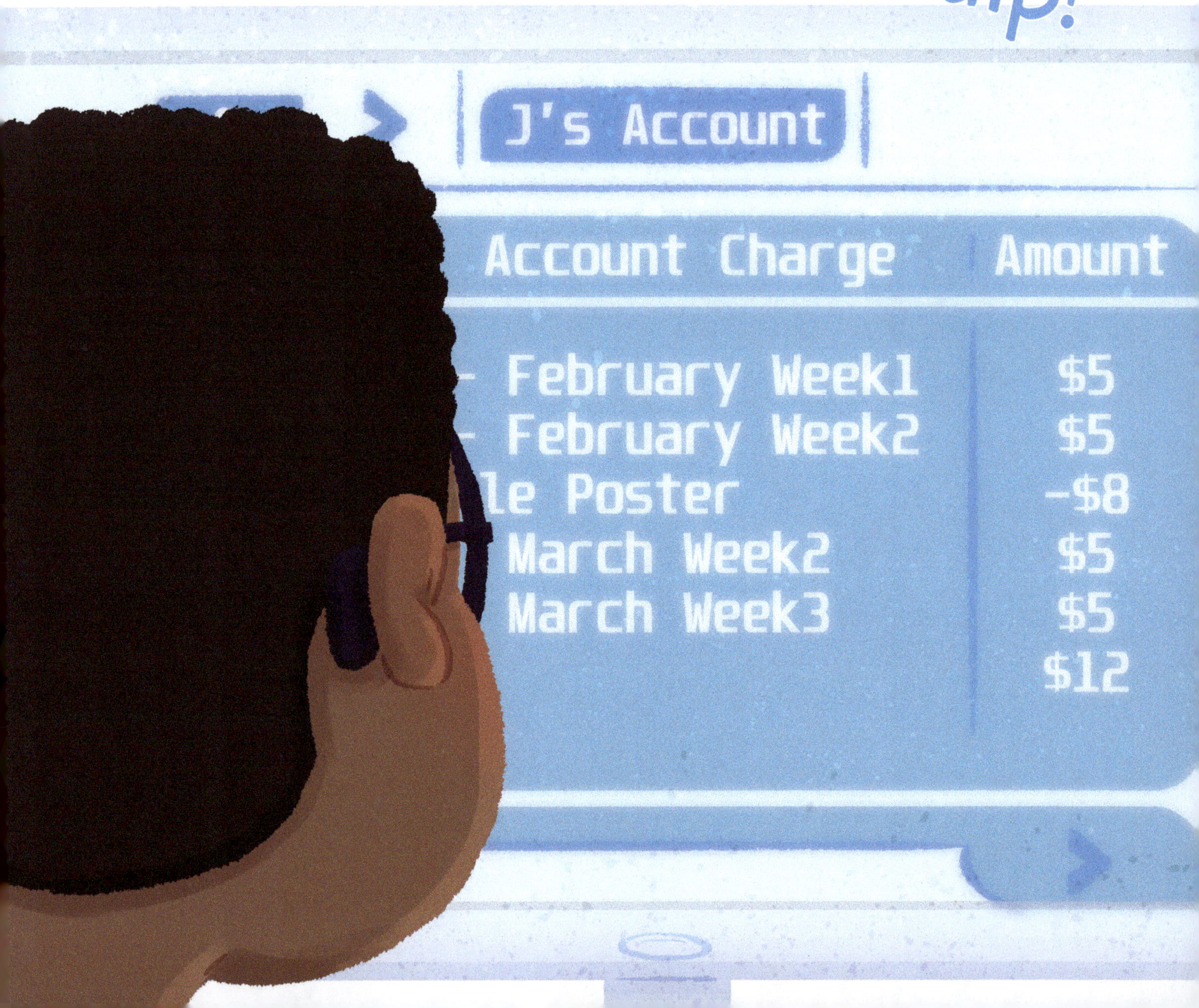

J's Account

Account Charge	Amount
February Week1	$5
February Week2	$5
le Poster	-$8
March Week2	$5
March Week3	$5
	$12

"Well, that's not enough!" pouts Joey. "Kass, I can't afford the camera, a video game, STEM camp, or anything! I really wanted to go to STEM camp! All my friends are going!"

Kass announces, "Yoo hoo...brother! Just look at your room. That's where all your money went. You seem to buy everything you see." SNAP!

Joey mutters, "Saving just doesn't flow well with my imagination or creativity."

"Does going to STEM Camp flow with your creativity?" asks Kass. Joey thinks about STEM Camp. He begins to worry.

"Imagine building a block tower 12 feet tall at STEM camp, or a remote-control robot, or even a volcano that really erupts! Is your imagination big enough for that? You don't need a camera. You need to dream of what YOU want, save your allowance, create a plan and stick to it! It's called making a budget."

"I never thought of it like that. So, I can save just by being creative and sticking to a budget?"

"Absolutely, and you can have a camera, a video game, STEM Camp or whatever you want in no time!" says Kass, as she snaps yet another picture. SNAP!

"So Joey, what's more important—the video game now or STEM Camp this summer?"

"Definitely STEM Camp!" says Joey, "and I don't like to say this, but I need your help, Kass."

"Okay," says Kass. "Your chores earn you 5 dollars a week. That adds up to 20 dollars each month. If you don't spend any of your monthly allowance, Dad and Mom give you an extra 10 dollar bonus. You could earn 30 dollars a month.

That adds up to 360 dollars a year! So, instead of buying video games, why not explore your dreams and save for the things you really want—like STEM Camp, new blocks, or even a mint-condition JazzCam Instant Camera like mine. Well of course, not mine!"

Joey doesn't have to think long before exclaiming, "Oh wow! That would be a lot of money! If I work and save my allowance, I will have enough money to pay the registration fee for STEM Camp. And Kass, I don't want your little camera."

"Now what's the plan for your budget, Joey?" Kass asks as she scans the room, looking at the vast array of games, posters, brightly colored T-shirts, and various toys.

Joey answers, "Well, I can create a savings goal to save for the things I really want. Maybe I don't need everything. Dad can even help me sell a few things so I can pay the camp registration fee sooner."

SNAP!

Joey begins working hard each week, completing his chores, and fighting the urge to buy new things.

His dad helps him sell some of his toys and posters at the neighborhood garage sale.

In two months, Joey saves enough money for STEM Camp! He and his friends are on their way to camp and he is proud of his accomplishment...

...and his room has never been cleaner.

Color in your savings goal. As you save, fill in how much you saved!

— 100%

— 75%

— 50%

— 25%

Savings Goal: $ 200

I am saving for toys a bonit, and a oufit

Learn more at www.createfinstew.com

Jasmine Paul is the author of A Boy, A Budget and a Dream. Her love for entrepreneurship sparked as she watched her grandmother own her seamstress business and became a shampoo girl in her aunt's salon. As a Certified Financial Education Instructor and money wellness leader, she hopes to empower youth and adults to have healthy money conversations early and often.
For creative money lessons visit createfinstew.com

About the Author

José Andrés Nieto is an artist with over five years of experience in the field of illustration as well as three published children's books. His academic background on digital platforms as Schoolism and SVS Learn, along with his knowledge in storyboard and comic art have allowed him to fuse his passion for graphic narrative and the colorful and playful nature of children's art, enabling him to visually create fun new stories for readers to explore. View Jose's portfolio: https://www.artstation.com/joseanieto

About the Illustrator

CPSIA information can be obtained
at www.ICGtesting.com
Printed in the USA
LVHW072135121021
700288LV00004B/24

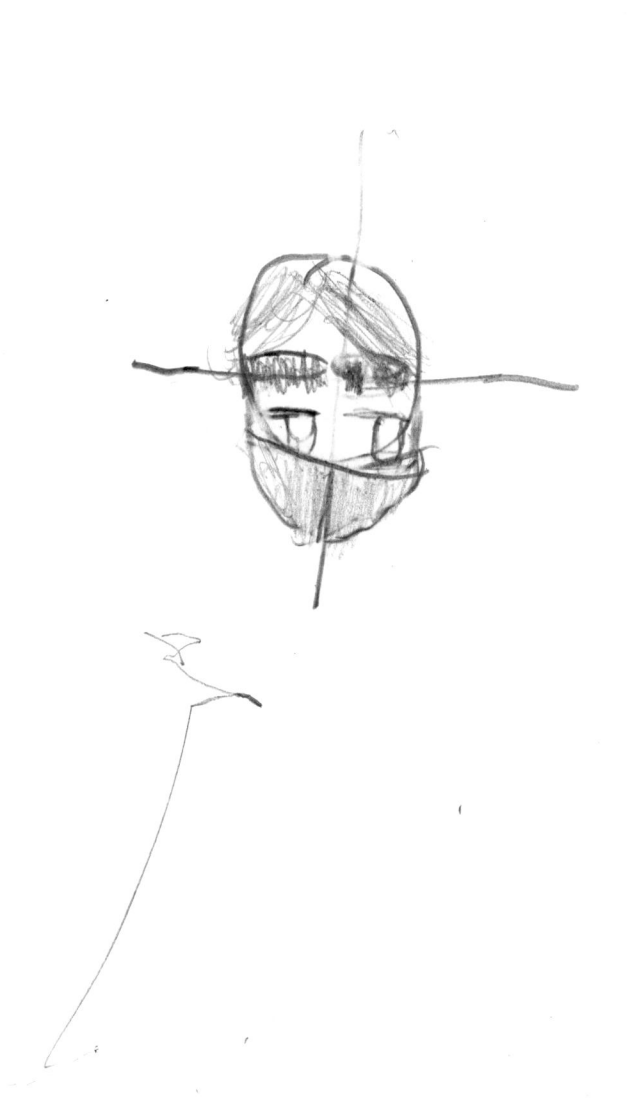